RAINFORESTS

Beautiful blue butterflies fly from flower to flower, and birds fly in and out of the tall trees. Jaguars wait silently in the shadows, and above them monkeys play. And around you there are hundreds, perhaps thousands of different flowers, plants, and trees – coffee, oranges, bananas, rice, and others that we do not have names for yet. It is hot and wet – rain falls around you, and clouds hide the tops of the trees. Yes, the rainforest is a wonderful, strange place.

But it is a place in great danger too. Every day people cut down its great trees to make farms, roads, and towns. Come with us to the rainforest and meet its people, its animals, and its plants. Read about the people who want to protect the rainforest – and the people who want to sell it and destroy it.

Come with us to the rainforest – before it disappears for ever . . .

T0364648

OXFORD BOOKWORMS LIBRARY
Factfiles

Rainforests
Stage 2 (700 headwords)

Factfiles Series Editor: Christine Lindop

ROWENA AKINYEMI

Rainforests

OXFORD UNIVERSITY PRESS

OXFORD
UNIVERSITY PRESS

Great Clarendon Street, Oxford OX2 6DP

Oxford University Press is a department of the University of Oxford.
It furthers the University's objective of excellence in research, scholarship,
and education by publishing worldwide in

Oxford New York

Auckland Cape Town Dar es Salaam Hong Kong Karachi
Kuala Lumpur Madrid Melbourne Mexico City Nairobi
New Delhi Shanghai Taipei Toronto

With offices in

Argentina Austria Brazil Chile Czech Republic France Greece
Guatemala Hungary Italy Japan Poland Portugal Singapore
South Korea Switzerland Thailand Turkey Ukraine Vietnam

OXFORD and OXFORD ENGLISH are registered trade marks of
Oxford University Press in the UK and in certain other countries

ISBN: 978 0 19 423381 1

A complete recording of this Bookworms edition of *Rainforests* is available

Printed in China

Word count (main text): 6480

For more information on the Oxford Bookworms Library,
visit www.oup.com/elt/bookworms

Illustration page 2 by Gareth Riddiford

The publishers would like to thank the following for permission to reproduce images:

Alamy Images pp 9 (temple/Imagestate), 10 (Yanomami girls/Sue Cunningham Photographic), 28
(burnt rainforest/Woodfall Wild Images), 30 (hydroelectric dam/Sue Cunningham Photographic);
FLPA pp 4 (butterfly/Frans Lanting), 13 (tapir/SA TEAM/FOTO NATURA), 16 (macaw/Pete Oxford/
Minden Pictures), 16 (tamarin/Jurgen & Christine Sohns), 21 (Rafflesia/Albert Visage); Getty Images
pp 8 (maize/SambaPhoto), 17 (quetzal/Kevin Schafer/Photographer's Choice), 17 (katydid/Brian
Kennedy/Taxi), 18 (butterfly/Gail Shumway/Taxi), 20 (bamboo/Anna Grossman/Photonica), 38
(Wangari Maathai/AFP); Lonely Planet Images pp 6 (rubber tapping/Wayne Walton), 36 (footbridge/
David Wall); National Geographic Image Collection p 31 (Dian Fossey/Peter G. Veit); Nature Picture
Library p 3 (sifaka/Pete Oxford); NHPA pp vii (trees/George Bernard), 12 (red howler monkeys/Lee Dalton), 14 (gorillas/Martin Harvey), 14 (otter/Andy Rouse),
15 (jaguar/Andy Rouse), 19 (mahogany tree/Martin Harvey), 24 (cattle/Martin Wendler), 26 (eroded
road/Bill Love), 34 (orangutan/Martin Harvey); Panos Pictures pp 22 (gold mine/Jeremy Horner),
40 (sapling/Dermot Tatlow); Reuters Pictures p 32 (Marina Silva/Jamil Bittar); South American
Pictures pp 25 (Trans Amazon highway/Tony Morrison), 25 (bulldozer working on Trans Amazon
highway/Marion Morrison).

CONTENTS

1 Rainforests

Rainforests are perhaps the most important places on earth. And yet we destroy thousands of square kilometres of rainforest every year. In 1950, rainforests covered 15 per cent of the earth's land. Fifty years later we have destroyed more than half of these rainforests. Will there still be any rainforests in the year 2050? No one knows the answer to that question. We must learn about the rainforests and try to protect them. We can use the rainforests *and* save them, too.

Rainforests are home to about fifty million people and millions of species of animals, plants, and insects. In one square kilometre of rainforest there can be more than 75,000 different species of trees. In all of Britain there are only 1,443 different species of plants. So when we destroy the rainforests thousands of species of plants and animals disappear, and forest people lose their homes.

The leaves of rainforest trees make about 40 per cent of the earth's oxygen. Can the earth live without the oxygen of the rainforests? What will happen to us when there are no more rainforests? We do not know – and let's hope that we never find out the answer!

The weather in a rainforest is hot all the year round – usually between 20 °C and 28 °C every day. The weather is always wet, too: rainforests have more than 200 millimetres of rain in a month. In Belém, in Brazil, it rains on about

243 days each year. And the rain is heavy! On a rainy day in a rainforest 20 millimetres of rain can fall. On a rainy day in London, about 5 millimetres of rain falls.

The largest rainforest in the world is the Amazon rainforest which grows in nine different countries in Latin America. The Amazon rainforest is about a hundred million years old, and has more species of animals and plants than any other place on earth. You can find 20 per cent of all the bird species in the world here. The great Amazon River, which runs through the Amazon rainforest, is the second longest river in the world. It runs 6,400 kilometres from the Andes Mountains to the Atlantic Ocean at Belém, in Brazil, where it is more than 300 kilometres across. There are more than 2,000 species of fish in the Amazon River, more than in all the Atlantic Ocean.

But this big rainforest is getting smaller. Between 1978 and 2004, more than half a million square kilometres of the Amazon rainforest disappeared.

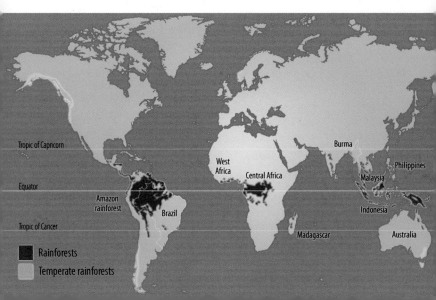

Tropic of Capricorn

Burma

West
Africa

Central Africa

Philippines

Malaysia

Equator

Amazon
rainforest

Brazil

Indonesia

Tropic of Cancer

Madagascar

Australia

▮ Rainforests
▮ Temperate rainforests

A sifaka can jump from one tree to another

The second largest rainforest is in Central Africa, and the world's ninth longest river, the Congo River, runs through it. There are also some rainforests in West Africa.

One part of the Central African rainforest is in Madagascar, which was once part of Africa. About 160 million years ago it moved away from Africa, and since that time it has been an island. Its animals and plants have changed very little in those years, and most of them live in no other place on earth. About fifty different species of lemur live in Madagascar and scientists are still finding new species. In Andohahela, there are twelve species of lemurs living in 760 square kilometres. The sifaka, a lemur with very long legs, can jump from one tree to another and travel a long way without touching the ground.

The third great rainforest is in southeast Asia, in Burma, Malaysia, Borneo, and Indonesia, and also in some of the islands of the South Pacific.

Between 1950 and 1995, Indonesia lost half of its

A Rajah Brooke's birdwing butterfly

rainforest. It sells most of the wood from its forest to rich countries. The Rajah Brooke's birdwing butterfly lives in these forests. It is one of the world's largest butterflies, with wings about 15 centimetres across. But Indonesia is destroying the home of this beautiful insect.

Australia has rainforests too, but they are disappearing fast. In 1988, someone found a new species of kangaroo in the rainforest of Australia. This was the Bennett's tree kangaroo. Most kangaroos live on the ground, but the Bennett's tree kangaroo, which has strong arms and wide feet, lives in trees. When the forests disappear, how many new species, like this kangaroo, disappear too? We cannot know.

Most rainforests grow on flat land, but some grow high in the mountains and are called cloud forests. Some rainforests grow by the sea, usually at the mouths of great rivers, where big trees called mangroves grow in the water. The biggest mangrove forests are in India and Bangladesh.

There are temperate rainforests too, which are wet, but not as hot as the rainforests in places like the Amazon. The temperate rainforest in North America grows in north California, and goes north by the Pacific Ocean, through Canada to Alaska. Rainfall in this forest can be more than 200 millimetres a month, and some of the trees grow 48 metres tall. Temperate rainforests also grow in Tasmania, Australia.

A Bennett's tree kangaroo

2 Why rainforests are important

More than half the species of plants and animals of the earth live in the rainforests, but we only know about a small number of them. We can learn more, but we must hurry.

People who live in the rainforests have always used plants to make medicines. Today, all over the world, people use medicines that are made from rainforest plants. Quinine, the medicine for malaria, comes from the cinchona tree of Peru. From the leaves of the beautiful Madagascan flower called the rosy periwinkle scientists make a medicine for the deadly blood disease leukaemia.

Many of the medicines that doctors use for cancer come from the rainforests. In the 1960s, scientists used

Rubber trees

a tree which grows in the temperate rainforest of North America to make a new medicine for cancer. Scientists use another plant, from the Sarawak rainforest in Borneo, as a medicine for cancer.

Many new medicines are waiting in the rainforests and scientists are trying to find them. If we destroy the rainforests we will never find them.

Rainforest trees give us many things which we use every day. Rubber, for example, comes from a rainforest tree, and some trees give us oil.

More than 3,000 kinds of fruits grow in the rainforests and many of them are good to eat. The people of the rainforests use more than 2,000 of them – the rest of the world eats only about 200 kinds. Two of the most popular fruits from the rainforests are bananas and oranges. And there are other rainforest food plants that people eat all over the world, for example coffee, tea, chocolate, and rice.

Maize, which is an important food for many people, is another rainforest plant. In 1970, a disease destroyed half the maize in the United States, so scientists began to look for new species of maize in the rainforests. In 1987, in the Mexican rainforest, they found a new species which is stronger than other species. But we nearly lost this new species of maize, because people were already cutting down that part of the Mexican rainforest.

Bananas too are in danger from disease. In the 1950s, a disease killed bananas in plantations in many countries. People then planted a new species of banana from the forests of China. But now a new disease is travelling

Maize is an important rainforest plant

across the world. Again, scientists have to look for another species of banana in the rainforests.

How many new species of useful plants have disappeared from the rainforests? Nobody knows.

The trees of the rainforest help the air because their leaves use carbon dioxide and make oxygen, which we need to live. They are important for the earth's weather too; water from their large leaves goes up into the sky and makes heavy clouds. The clouds then give rain back to the rainforests, and some clouds move to other parts of the earth and give rain there. The clouds also protect the earth from the sun.

Today, the earth is slowly getting hotter, and in some places changes in the weather mean that life is much more difficult for millions of people. We need to learn more about the earth's weather while we still have the rainforests.

3

People of the rainforests

Many years ago, there were large cities and gardens in some rainforests. In Nigeria, scientists found old walls 10 metres high. These walls were built around a town in the rainforest more than a thousand years ago. In the Mexican rainforest, the Mayan people built great stone buildings, and in the rainforest of Cambodia there are hundreds of buildings at Angkor. In both places there are buildings that are more than a thousand years old.

Today, about fifty million people live in the rainforests of the world and most of them do not damage the forest that they live in. They take the fruit from the forest trees,

Angkor, Cambodia

but they do not cut the trees down. They kill some animals to eat, but they do not destroy the species.

When we cut down the rainforests, we destroy the lives of these forest people too. In 1900, there were one million forest people in the Amazon forest. In 1980, there were only 200,000.

The Yanomami live along the rivers of the rainforest in the north of Brazil. They have lived in the rainforest for more than 10,000 years and they use more than 2,000 different plants for food and for medicine. But in 1988, someone found gold in their forest, and suddenly 45,000 people came to the forest and began looking

Yanomani children

for gold. They cut down the forest to make roads. The Yanomami people lost land and food. Many died because new diseases came to the forest with the strangers.

The Yanomami people tried to save their forest, because it was their home. But the people who wanted gold were stronger, and many of the Yanomami people lost their homes. In 1992, Brazil made a national park for the Yanomami people. A national park (or forest park) is a safe place for plants and animals; people cannot make towns or cut down trees there. So now the Yanomami have a home which is safe.

The Enawene Nawe people live in Mato Grosso in Brazil. There are only 420 of these people. They eat fish and fruits which they find in the forest. They want to protect their forest because they are in danger from big soya businesses.

Many forest people try to save their forests. Chico Mendes was famous in Brazil and all over the world because he wanted to keep the forest for his people. 'I want the Amazon forest to help all of us – forest people, Brazil, and all the earth,' he said. Chico Mendes was born in the rainforest, and when he was still a child he began working on a rubber plantation with his father. In 1976 he began to work with other rubber workers to protect the rainforests. Businesses were buying the forest of the rubber workers, and Chico Mendes told people in Brazil and other countries about the disappearing forests. In 1988, people who wanted to cut down the forest murdered Chico Mendes outside his home.

In Borneo, people began to cut down the forest of the Penan people to sell the wood. The Penan people tried to save their rainforest. In 1987 they closed fifteen roads into the forest for eight months. No one cut down any trees during that time. The organization Survival International began working with the Penan people in the 1970s, and is still helping them and their forest.

The Gavioes people of Brazil use the forest, but they protect it too. They find and sell the Brazil nuts which grow on the Brazil nut forest trees. These trees grow high above the other rainforest trees in the Amazon and they can live for 1,000 years. The Brazil nut tree will not grow on plantations, so only the forest people can find and sell the nuts.

4   Rainforest animals

Many different species of animals and plants live in the rainforests. Some are strange, some are beautiful, and some are very new – to us.

A lot of rainforest animals live in the tops of the trees. There is a lot of food here, so some animals never go down to the forest floor. This part of the forest is called the canopy, and scientists began to learn about it in the 1980s. At first they climbed the trees like mountain climbers. Now they have cameras that can move through the canopy and take photographs.

Howler monkeys live in the canopy of the Amazon rainforest. They are the loudest monkeys in the world,

Howler monkeys

and they howl (scream loudly) in the morning and at night. When they howl, they are calling other groups of monkeys, and you can hear their cries 5 kilometres away. The howler monkeys eat leaves, and a lot of the time they sleep in the trees.

But many animals are in danger because we are destroying their homes. Tapirs live near rivers in the forests of Latin America and Malaysia. They are about

A tapir

three metres long, and can be as heavy as a horse. It is not easy to see a tapir because they spend the hot hours of the day in the river. At night, they come out to eat leaves. We know that tapirs were already living in the rainforests twenty million years

ago. But when the rainforest gets smaller, the number of tapirs in the world gets smaller too.

The Javan rhinoceros once lived in the rainforests of many countries: in the north of India, through Indo-China, and south through Malaysia and the islands of Indonesia. But today there are only about sixty of these animals in the world; some live in Vietnam and some live in the Ujung Kulon National Forest Park on the island of Java, where park workers protect them.

In forest parks people can visit and watch the animals, but they cannot kill them. Today there are many forest

Mountain gorillas

parks in the rainforests of the world. Many of them are large, because some species have to travel many kilometres to find food. The Parc National des Volcans in Rwanda, Africa, for example, is 120 square kilometres, and is home to the mountain gorilla. Mountain gorillas live in family groups and are very big, so they don't climb trees very often. They spend most of the time on the ground and they need to eat lots of leaves and fruit. Workers in the forest park try to protect these big, slow animals.

The biggest danger to many animals is people. People want the animals for their fur, or for their meat, or they want to sell the animals as pets. Giant otters live in the Amazon rainforest. They are about 2 metres long, and they sleep in deep holes by the river. Giant otters live in family groups, and a group of otters will eat more than 30,000 fish a year. There are only about 100 giant

A giant otter

otters now, because people will pay a lot of money for their beautiful, thick fur. In the 1960s, people killed more than 60,000 giant otters in Brazil.

Jaguars are the largest and strongest cats of the Latin American rainforests. They are good swimmers, and eat tapirs, fish, otters, and other animals. The word jaguar means 'someone who kills with one jump'. The rainforest

A jaguar

people do not kill these cats, but other people come to the forests and kill jaguars for their beautiful black and gold fur.

The hyacinth macaw is a beautiful, big, noisy blue bird. They live in Brazil, Paraguay, and Bolivia. There are only about 2,500 wild birds, but people are still catching hyacinth macaws and selling them in pet shops. Some people who once caught hyacinth macaws are now learning about these birds and protecting them.

Zoos in many countries of the world are helping to

A hyacinth macaw

A golden lion tamarin

protect animals in danger. The golden lion tamarin is a very rare monkey which comes from Brazil's forest near the Atlantic Ocean. People took hundreds of these monkeys from the forest and sold them to pet shops, or killed them for their soft golden fur. In the 1970s, there were only about 200 golden lion tamarins in the rainforest. But many were born in zoos, and scientists have taken some of them back to the Poco das Antas Forest Park near Rio de Janeiro. Now about 1,200 tamarins live in the forest.

Animals that are born in zoos know nothing about life in the rainforests. Someone must teach them to find food and to keep away from danger. Janis Carter teaches chimpanzees about life in the rainforest of The Gambia because they were born in zoos far away from the forest. In Borneo, scientist Biruté Galdikas teaches young orang-utans about life in the forest.

Then there are the rainforest birds. One rainforest park in Peru has more species of birds than are found in all the United States.

The quetzal is a large green and red bird, about one metre long, which eats only fruit. The quetzal lives in the

A quetzal

mountain rainforests from Mexico to Costa Rica. It can find some kind of fruit here every day of the year. If you take a quetzal out of the forest, it will die.

Other rainforest birds eat only insects. And there are hummingbirds, very small beautiful birds that get their food from flowers. While they do this, their wings move up and down about fifty-five times every second.

A leaf katydid

No one knows all the species of insects in the rainforests. Perhaps there are more than 40,000 species of insects in the Amazon rainforest. The leaf katydid is one of these. It looks like the leaf that it is standing on. In this way it protects itself from the birds in the trees around it.

In the Manu National Park in Peru there are more than 1,200 species of butterfly. All of Europe has only about 320 species of butterfly. Queen Alexandra's Birdwing is the biggest butterfly in the world, with wings about 30 centimetres across. This butterfly lives in the rainforest of Papua New Guinea. The bright blue Morpho butterfly, with wings about 15 centimetres across, lives in the rainforests of Latin America. Baby jaguars try to catch and eat these butterflies.

We will never know about some animals that live in the rainforests, because every year about a thousand different species disappear for ever.

A Morpho butterfly

5 Rainforest plants

The rainforests are as rich in plants as they are in animals. The biggest plants are of course the trees, and they are 70 per cent of the plants in the rainforests. The island of Madagascar has 2,000 species of trees. In all of North America there are only 700 species of trees.

Rainforest trees grow very slowly, and they live for hundreds of years. When a mahogany tree is fifteen years old it is about 15 metres tall. After fifty years, it is about 30 metres. It goes on growing until it is 150 years old. Now scientists know that many rainforest trees are more than 300 years old, and some trees in the Amazon rainforest are more than 1,000 years old.

A mahogany tree

Some trees grow as tall as 70 metres – and some animals live all their lives in the top of these trees! The tallest trees in the rainforests have small leaves. The rain falls off the leaves quickly so they do not get too heavy. But the smaller trees have large leaves to get as much light from the sun as possible. Down on the forest floor it is dark, and few plants can grow there. People can easily walk through most parts of an old rainforest.

In the Asian rainforest, one of the most important plants is bamboo. Bamboo grows up to 25 metres tall and lives for twenty-five to forty years. Bamboo needs a lot of water to grow, and without bamboo, the heavy forest rains carry the soil away. People make floors, tables, chairs, and paper from bamboo.

One famous tree is the petroleum nut tree, from the Philippines. People can burn the oil from the tree to cook their food or light their houses. One of these trees can make fifty litres of oil every year.

The physic nut tree has grown in the rainforests for 70 million years, and rainforest people use this small tree for medicine. Now people are using it for oil. After the oil is made, they use the rest of the tree for animal food. One

Bamboo

Rafflesia

plantation in Nicaragua has more than one million trees.

The rainforest is home to the largest flower in the world. It is called the rafflesia, and it grows in the forest on the island of Borneo. It can be as heavy as 10 kilos, and it can be more than 1 metre across. It smells terrible – like old dead meat!

In the cloud forests of Ecuador, scientists are finding many new orchids. Warm clouds nearly always cover these rainforests, and these very small beautiful flowers grow high in the forest canopy. But many rainforest plants, like the orchids, are in danger. People take the flowers or the plants to sell. If the plants are rare, they can get a lot of money for them.

6   Money

Why are we destroying the rainforests? There is a short answer to that question: money!

Countries with rainforests cut down about 50,000 square kilometres of trees every year, and sell the wood to rich countries. Most rainforest wood from Latin America goes to North America; wood from Africa goes to Europe; and wood from the forests of Asia goes to China and Japan. There are many forests in Japan, but Japan does not cut down the trees which grow in Japan. About 80 per cent of the wood which Japan uses comes from other countries. And the United States spends more than any other country on wood from rainforests.

Looking for gold, Colombia

Some countries have stopped buying rainforest wood. Switzerland stopped buying rainforest wood in 1982. Has your country stopped buying rainforest wood?

When people look for metals in the rainforest they also destroy the forests. When they take gold from the ground, they use deadly mercury to wash the gold. The mercury goes into the rivers and kills fish and other animals.

International businesses buy rainforests in Latin America where land is very cheap. They cut down the trees, sell the wood, and then use the land for cows. Then 90 per cent of the meat from the cows goes to North America. The meat is cheap – but what does it really cost? Trees and animals die, and forest people lose their homes, to make cheap meat for rich countries.

Animals need a lot of food and much more water than plants. To make 1 kilo of meat you need more than 40,000 litres of water. But 1 kilo of potatoes needs only 198 litres of water to grow. Even rice does not need as much water as meat.

All over the world, people eat 140 million tonnes of meat every year. The richest countries eat 60 per cent of this meat. For example, in Nigeria each person eats about 6.4 kilos of meat every year. In China, each person eats about 23 kilos. But in Europe and North America, each person eats over 60 kilos of meat every year.

Animals eat more than 30 per cent of the world's plant food. Brazil is destroying rainforests to make plantations of soya that it can sell for animal food. In 2005, Brazil grew more soya than any other country and China bought most of it for animal food.

Cows on rainforest land

Many countries have also cut down rainforests and planted coffee or sugar which they can sell to rich countries. Farmers keep insects, birds, and animals out of coffee, sugar, or soya plantations because they do not want damage to the plants. They use chemicals to kill the insects, and these chemicals damage the soil and give people cancer.

Organic plantations grow plants without chemicals. Organic coffee grows under the tall trees of the rainforest, and the birds in the trees eat the insects that damage the coffee. Families grew coffee like this before the big businesses cut down the trees and made large plantations of coffee. On a big plantation, you can see between five and twenty species of birds. On an organic coffee farm, you can see about 150 species of birds. Now there are more and more organic coffee farms in the rainforests, and workers have a better life without the chemicals of the big plantations.

7 Disappearing forests

About one per cent of all the rainforest in the world disappears every year. We know this from photographs which give us a true picture of the rainforests. We can see that great parts of the forest have disappeared in Brazil. Photographs tell us, for example, that between 1978 and 1988, people destroyed 170,000 square kilometres of rainforest in the Amazon, and from 2001 to 2002, about 25,000 square kilometres of Brazil's rainforest disappeared. Most of it is for soya plantations for animals in China, North America and Europe.

When roads are made through the rainforests, people start to destroy the forests very quickly. They can travel easily along the big roads to new parts of the forest. They use the roads to take away wood, and to bring in plants for plantations. Soon after the plantations come houses and farms.

Building a road

A new road

A road in Madagascar

The rainforests are full of trees and animals, but the soil is poor. This is because it is very old, and because all the good things that are in the soil move quickly into the trees and plants. Without the trees, the heavy rain washes away the soil and nothing can grow there again.

Look at the picture of the road in Madagascar. Once there was rainforest here, and now it is gone. But the rain that gave life to the trees has destroyed the road. People cut down the rainforest to make a road that nobody can use.

In the Amazon rainforest, there are four months every year when the wood businesses cut down the great trees and burn them to make a place for plantations. The great tauari and macaranduba trees burn for more than two years because they are so big. While the trees are burning, they make lots of carbon dioxide. Each year, burning the rainforests makes about 30 per cent of all carbon dioxide in the world. Because of this, the earth is getting hotter and the weather is changing.

In many rainforest countries, there are too many people in the cities, and many people move to the rainforests to grow food for themselves. For example, in 1960 there were about 10,000 people (most of them forest people) in Rondonia, in the west of Brazil. In the 1970s, Brazil asked people to move from the cities into Rondonia, until in 2004 1.5 million people were living there. These people need food, houses, and roads – and the cities of Rondonia grow while the rainforest gets smaller.

By about 2010 there will be no more rainforests in Indonesia. International paper businesses are destroying most of them. Indonesia asks the businesses to plant other trees for paper, but between 1988 and 2000, only 10 per cent of the wood came from plantations. The rest of the wood came from rainforest trees.

In the forests of Borneo there is a special tree called ramin. People make beautiful tables and chairs from the wood of this tree. Most of the wood goes to Italy. This tree will soon disappear, because Europe likes the wood so much.

Oil palm plantations are destroying other parts of Indonesia's rainforests. The oil palm tree comes from the West African rainforest but now Indonesia and Malaysia make most of the world's palm oil. Look at the food in your supermarket, and you will see that we use palm oil to make many things. There are plans for one new oil palm plantation in Indonesia which will destroy between 18,000 and 20,000 square kilometres of rainforest.

In 1997, the burning of forests in Indonesia made great clouds of smoke that covered much of Malaysia. Every year since then, smoke from the forest fires has made trouble for the people of Malaysia. In August 2005, schools and airports in Malaysia closed because smoke from forest fires came across the sea to the cities in Malaysia. More than 900 fires were burning. Newspapers told people to stay in their homes because the smoke was dangerous.

Burning rainforest

Without the rainforests there are more floods in the world. In 1920, rainforests covered 62 per cent of the Philippines. Most of this forest has gone, and in 2004 the forests covered only 18 per cent of the country. Without the forest trees, the heavy rain does not go down deep into the ground; it runs quickly into the rivers and sometimes covers many square kilometres of ground. In 2004, hundreds of people died in the Philippines because of terrible floods.

East Africa does not have much rain now, because the forests have gone. Rainforest trees take water from the ground and through their leaves water moves into the clouds and falls as rain. Without the trees, there is less

The Itaipu Dam, between Brazil and Paraguay

rain and hotter weather. More countries in Africa now have the deadly disease malaria because the weather is hotter.

In Latin America, many countries want to build dams to make more electricity for their cities. But when a new dam is built, the water behind it covers many square kilometres. For example, with money from North America and Europe, Brazil is building dams in the Amazon rainforest. These dams will make 40 per cent of Brazil's electricity. Already, two dams have destroyed 4,400 square kilometres of forest.

In Australia, too, the rainforest is in danger. Many people were angry when the government wanted to destroy a lot of rainforest in Northern Queensland and build a dam on the Tully River. In the end, the dam was not built. But how long will the rainforest be safe?

Scientists know other ways to make electricity; for example, you can use the sun or the wind. Many countries, and some rainforest countries, are now beginning to use these new ways to make electricity. So there is a little bit of hope for the rainforests.

8 Protectors of the rainforests

Many people and organizations in different countries work to help the people, animals, and plants of the rainforest.

Dian Fossey moved to Rwanda in 1967, and began to learn about the mountain gorillas there. She lived in Rwanda for eighteen years, and she learned a lot about the gorillas and their quiet family life. When people killed one of her favourite gorillas, she began to speak against people who killed gorillas for food and fur. She wrote a famous book about the gorillas, called *Gorillas in the Mist*, and this book was later made into a film. Someone murdered Dian Fossey in 1985, but her organization, the Gorilla Fund, still works with the gorillas in Rwanda.

Dian Fossey with gorillas

In 1990, Ian and Karen McAllister began fighting for the Great Bear Rainforest in Canada. More than half the trees that people cut down in this old forest go to the United States. The McAllisters want to stop this and to protect the animals and trees of this forest. Their organization is called the Raincoast Conservation Society, and the McAllisters have written a book about the forest called *The Great Bear Rainforest*.

Marina Silva worked with Chico Mendes and the forest people who worked on the rubber plantations. She was born in 1961 in the Amazon rainforest, and worked there on the rubber trees with her father. She is often ill because of the poisonous metals in the rivers near her home; people who are looking for gold leave these metals there. After the murder of Chico Mendes, Marina Silva went on working with the rainforest people to make

Marina Silva

plantations which did not destroy the rainforests. She is famous in Brazil for her work for the rainforests and their people. In 2003 President Lula of Brazil made her Brazil's first Environment Minister.

In 2006 Brazil brought a new part of the rainforest into its Amazon National Park, which is now 458,000 square kilometres. This new part is near Anapu, which was the home of Sister Dorothy Stang for more than thirty years.

She worked with hundreds of forest families in their fight against big businesses which were cutting down the forests. In 2005, people who did not like her work murdered Sister Dorothy, who was seventy-four years old. After her death, Brazil stopped everyone cutting trees in that part of the forest.

In Kenya, as much as 90 per cent of the rainforests has gone, and many forest animals and plants have disappeared. Wangari Maathai began planting trees in 1977. She wanted to save the forest people and their land. Her organization, the Green Belt Movement, has planted more than 30 million trees. Since 1986 she has helped other African countries to begin organizations like hers. She is also starting coffee plantations which do not damage the forests. Wangari Maathai is now famous all over the world because of her work with trees. She thinks that every person in the world must help the earth.

Scientist Biruté Galdikas went to the rainforest of Borneo more than thirty years ago and began to learn about the orang-utans there. She lives in Tanjung Puting, which is now a national park. Orang-utans live only in Sumatra and Borneo, and between 1995 and 2005 over half of all orang-utans disappeared. People killed them for their meat or their fur, or they died in forest fires. Sometimes people take orang-utans from the forest and sell them to pet shops in other countries. Biruté Galdikas started the Orangutan Foundation International in 1986, and has written a book called *Reflections of Eden*.

The singer Sting and his wife Trudie Styler began the Rainforest Foundation in 1989 to help the rainforests

Orang-utans

and their people. The Foundation helped the Kayapo people who wanted to save their forest in Brazil. In 1993, Brazil gave the Kayapo people 44,030 square kilometres of forest. The Foundation also helps rainforest people in other countries in Latin America, Africa, and Asia.

In Australia, there are many organizations that help the rainforests. Big paper businesses are cutting down the old forests of Tasmania, but now many Australians are trying to save these forests.

Survival International helps rainforest people in many countries. The World Wildlife Fund (WWF) works with rainforest countries and protects rare animals that are losing their rainforest homes. Greenpeace is also working with forest people, for example in the Paradise rainforests of Asia. In 2006, the Greenpeace ship *Rainbow Warrior* arrived in Papua New Guinea to help the Kuni people. They want to save their forest, which is disappearing fast.

9 Tourists in the rainforests

Visitors can destroy the rainforests and their people and animals. But they can help them too. Now there are new ways to bring people and the rainforests together.

In 2003, Madagascar made its National Park bigger. The forests of the National Park now cover 10 per cent of the country. If the people of Madagascar protect the forests, tourists will visit the country and see the wonderful animals, birds and plants. Having tourists means money and jobs that people really need in one of the poorest countries in the world.

Many tourists visit the Parc National des Volcans in Rwanda. This park was Dian Fossey's home while she lived with the mountain gorillas. Now you can stay in a hotel at the bottom of one of the six mountains in the park. You can walk through the bamboo forest, and see golden monkeys, some of the park's 650 species of birds, and 100 species of orchids. After you have walked for about four hours, you will find a group of gorillas. You can watch them while they eat, play, and rest.

Panama, in Latin America, has lost more than half of its forests. But the Kuna people saved their forest. They made a forest park which tourists pay to visit. They have built a hotel on a mountain in Nusagandi, and they show

Tourists visiting
the rainforest

tourists the birds and plants of the forest. The tourists learn about the rainforest and the Kuna people can stay in their forest.

Tourists can visit many places in the rainforests of Latin America. You can visit the Madidi National Park in Bolivia, or the Pico da Neblina National Park in Brazil, and learn about the animals and plants of the forest. In Peru, you can visit the Manu National Park, and see tapirs, giant otters, monkeys, butterflies, and thousands of birds. You can travel on a boat on the Amazon River and see the villages of the forest people. Or you can visit an organic coffee plantation.

In Malaysia, there are more than 1,000 species of butterflies. At the Penang Butterfly Farm more than 120 species fly around their favourite flowers, and tourists enjoy watching these beautiful insects.

In Costa Rica, a rainforest tree business has planted nearly two million rainforest trees. People from many countries are buying their own rainforest trees, and many tourists are visiting these trees.

Many people from different countries would like to work in the rainforests. You can work with the giant otters, or the hyacinth macaws. You can help to grow rainforest bananas in Costa Rica. You can plant trees in Kenya with Wangari Maathai's Green Belt Movement, and visit her learning centre near Nairobi.

And you do not always have to go to rainforest countries to see rainforests. In Britain you can visit the Eden Project, in Cornwall, or the Royal Botanic Gardens at Kew, near London. In these places you can see many rainforest plants and learn about the work that scientists are doing with them. At the Eden Project plants and trees grow in special houses called 'biomes'. On a cold grey day you can go into the biome and walk through a hot, wet rainforest – in Britain!

Wangari Maathai planting a tree

10 How you can help the rainforests

All of us, in every country of the world, must try to help and save the rainforests. Here are some things you can do.

- Learn about the rainforests and tell other people about them.
- Buy 'tree-free' paper – paper that is not made from wood.
- Use paper that is made from old paper – this saves trees.
- Buy organic coffee, chocolate, and bananas.
- Buy Brazil nuts!
- Eat less meat.
- When you go to the supermarket, look for things that do not have palm oil in them.

If you want to help the rainforests, do not buy these things:

- anything that is made from the fur of a rainforest animal
- any rainforest animal for a pet
- anything that is made from rainforest wood
- gold from rainforest countries
- meat from Latin America
- rainforest flowers or plants, or flowers from plantations in rainforest countries

Everyone on earth must help the rainforests
if we want oxygen and water for our children.
We cannot wait for other people and other
countries – we must start today!

GLOSSARY

air what you breathe

cancer a dangerous illness that can make people very ill or kill them

carbon dioxide the gas that people breathe out

chemical something solid or liquid that is made by chemistry

cover *(v)* to be all over something

cut down to cut something so that it falls down

dam a wall that is built across a river to hold the water back

damage to break or harm something

destroy when something is destroyed, it is dead and finished (e.g. fire destroys a forest)

disappear to go away from a place; to stop existing

disease an illness

earth the world

electricity power that can make heat and light

flood when there is a flood, a lot of water covers the land

fur the soft thick hair on animals

giant very big

grow to get bigger; (of a plant) to live somewhere; to plant something in the ground and look after it

insect a very small animal that has six legs

international connected with two or more countries

kind a group of things that are the same in some way

malaria a serious disease that you get from the bite of a small insect

medicine something to eat or drink that helps you to get better when you are ill

mercury a dangerous silver-coloured liquid metal

metal   something solid that is usually hard and shiny; iron and gold are metals

oil   a thick liquid that comes from a plant and is used for cooking or light or heating

organic   grown in a natural way, without using chemicals

organization   a group of people who work together for a special purpose

oxygen   a gas in the air that people and animals need to live

part   one of the pieces of something

pet   an animal that you keep in your home

plant (*n & v*)   something that grows in the ground; to put a plant in the ground

plantation   a big piece of land where things like sugar or bananas grow

poisonous   something that is poisonous will kill you or make you very ill if you eat or drink it

protect   to keep something safe

rare   if something is rare, you do not see or find it often

rubber   something that comes from trees and is used to make car tyres, boots etc.

save   to take something away from danger, or to take away the things that are a danger to something

scientist   a person who studies natural things

soil   what plants and trees grow in

soya   a plant grown as food for people and animals

species   a group of animals that are the same in some way

tourist   a person who visits a place on holiday

zoo   a place where you can see wild animals in a town or city

Rainforests

ACTIVITIES

ACTIVITIES

Before Reading

1 **Read the introduction on the first page of the book, and the back cover. What do you know now about the rainforests? Are these sentences true (T) or false (F)?**

1 It is hot and wet in the rainforests.

2 In 1950 half of the world's rainforests disappeared.

3 We know everything about the plants and trees in the rainforests.

4 People want to use the land of the rainforests for towns and roads.

5 People use fire to destroy the rainforest trees.

6 People cut down rainforest trees to make houses for themselves.

7 We have a lot of time to save the rainforests.

8 Some animals are dying because people are destroying the rainforests.

2 **Can you guess the numbers? Choose one answer for each question.**

1 The leaves of rainforest trees make _____ per cent of the earth's oxygen.

   a) 20   b) 30   c) 40   d) 50

2 Rainforests are home to _____ million people.

   a) 50   b) 100   c) 200   d) 250

3 Rainforest people use more than _____ kinds of fruit.

   a) 200   b) 1,000   c) 1,500   d) 2,000

ACTIVITIES

While Reading

Read Chapters 1, 2, and 3. Are these sentences true (T) or false (F)?

1 In most rainforests it is usually hotter than 20 °C.

2 The Amazon rainforest is getting bigger.

3 Scientists have named all the different species of lemur in Madagascar.

4 There are rainforests on mountains.

5 Quinine is made from the rosy periwinkle.

6 Rainforest people use more kinds of fruit than other people do.

7 Bananas are a popular fruit from the rainforest.

8 Rainforest trees are important because their leaves make carbon dioxide.

9 Most rainforest people do not cut down rainforest trees.

10 Since 1992 the Yanomami people have had a safe place to live.

11 Chico Mendes died because he cut down too many rainforest trees.

12 Some of the Gavioes people are more than 1,000 years old.

Read Chapters 4 and 5, then complete the sentences with words from the list below.

bamboo, gorillas, howler monkeys, hyacinth macaws, jaguars, leaf katydid, mahogany trees, quetzals, rafflesia

1 You can hear _____ from 5 kilometres away.

2 _____ live mostly on the ground and move slowly.

3 _____ have beautiful black and gold fur.

4 _____ are big, blue, and beautiful.

5 _____ can always find fruit in the mountain rainforests.

6 The _____ looks like part of a plant.

7 _____ keep growing for 150 years.

8 _____ can be used for paper, floors, and chairs.

9 The _____ flower smells like a dead animal.

Read Chapters 6 and 7. Choose the best question-words for these questions and then answer them.

How / Where / Which / Who / Why

1 _____ country spends the most on rainforest wood?

2 _____ is looking for gold bad for rainforest fish and animals?

3 _____ eats more meat – a person in China or a person in North America?

4 _____ do farmers use chemicals on their plantations?

5 _____ is the soil poor in rainforests?

6 _____ do fires in rainforests change the weather?

7 _____ are fires in Indonesia a problem for Malaysia?

8 _____ country has had floods because the rainforests have gone?

9 _____ have dams destroyed thousands of square kilometres of rainforest?

Read Chapter 8. Then match the people with the descriptions.

Biruté Galdikas, Dian Fossey, Dorothy Stang,
Marina Silva, Sting and Trudie Styler, Wangari Maathai

1 _____ started an organization that protects gorillas.

2 _____ has an important job protecting the rainforest in Brazil.

3 _____ was killed after thirty years' work in the rainforest.

4 _____ plants trees in African countries.

5 _____ wants to save orang-utans.

6 _____ helped the Kayapo people.

Read Chapters 9 and 10, then match these halves of sentences.

1 In the Parc National des Volcans . . .

2 The Kuna people built a hotel for tourists . . .

3 In the Manu National Park . . .

4 At the Penang Butterfly Farm . .

5 If you want a rainforest tree . . .

6 At the Eden Project in Britain . . .

7 If you need to buy paper . . .

8 If you want a pet . . .

a look for paper that is 'tree-free'.

b you can see tapirs and otters.

c rainforest plants grow in biomes.

d you can watch gorillas play.

e you can see 120 species of beautiful insects.

f and they take them to see the rainforest.

g do not buy a rainforest animal.

h you can buy one in Costa Rica.

ACTIVITIES

After Reading

1 **Here is an interview between Wangari Maathai and a reporter. Put their conversation in order, and write in the speakers' names. The reporter speaks first (number 4).**

1 _____ 'And what changes has that made?'

2 _____ 'Now I am starting some new coffee plantations. They use no chemicals, so they do not damage the forests. And tourists can come to spend their holidays with us, planting trees.'

3 _____ 'And how many has the movement planted now?'

4 _____ 'What happened to the rainforests in Kenya?'

5 _____ 'I planted my first trees in 1977. That was the beginning of the Green Belt Movement.'

6 _____ 'Thank you very much, Wangari Maathai.'

7 _____ ' Once there were lots of rainforests, but now 90 per cent of them have gone.'

8 _____ 'Finally, you are a famous person now. What would you like to say to the people of the world?'

9 _____ 'Without the trees, we get less rain, and the weather gets hotter. Then life gets very difficult for the rainforest people.'

10 _____ '30 million – and now other African countries have organizations like ours too.'

11 _____ 'So you decided to help them. What did you do?'

12 _____ 'What new things are you doing now?'

13 _____ 'I think that everybody in the world must work to help the earth – every one of us.'

2 Find these words in the wordsearch below, and draw lines
through them. The words go from left to right, and from
top to bottom.

*cancer, dam, destroy, disappear, earth, electricity, flood, fur,
kind, mercury, metal, pet, poisonous, save, scientist, soil,
species, zoo*

D	E	S	T	R	O	Y	I	D	A	M
I	W	A	Z	S	E	N	T	T	H	E
S	E	A	O	C	A	N	C	E	R	R
A	M	A	O	I	R	Z	S	O	N	C
P	F	O	P	E	T	R	P	E	S	U
P	F	T	T	N	H	O	E	K	H	R
E	L	E	C	T	R	I	C	I	T	Y
A	O	S	O	I	L	E	I	N	F	L
R	O	P	A	S	A	V	E	D	U	L
L	D	M	E	T	A	L	S	O	R	F
U	P	O	I	S	O	N	O	U	S	S

Now write down all the letters that do not have lines through
them, beginning with the first line and going across each
line to the end. You now have 33 letters, which make a
sentence of 10 words.

1 What is the sentence, and who said it?
2 Why was he famous?
3 What happened to him?

3 Complete these two newspaper reports from the year 2012,
   using the words below (one word for each gap). The two
   headlines also need one word from each list.

   birds, businesses, dangerous, destroy, disappeared, enjoying,
   films, fires, great, happy, inside, money, paper, pay, plant,
   plantations, reporters, save, scientists, species, stay, trouble,
   unhappy, wood

1

_____ day for the rainforest

HERE in Indonesia the rainforest has now _____.
International _____ took the _____ to make _____,
but they did not _____ other trees. And oil palm
_____ have helped to _____ the rainforest too.
Only the people of Malaysia can feel _____ today.
Now there will be no more _____ from the smoke
of forest _____. They will not have to stay _____
because of the _____ smoke.

2

_____ day for the rainforest

_____ in Madagascar said today that they have found three new _____ of lemur. They showed _____ of the animals to _____ at the Forest Park Hotel. _____ from the hotel helps to _____ for the scientists' work. Tourists who _____ at the hotel can visit the rainforest and see animals, _____ and plants.

'I'm really _____ my holiday,' said one visitor today. 'It's good that some of the money from my holiday is helping to _____ the animals of the rainforest.'

Which of these articles do you think you will see in the
newspaper in 2012? Why do you think this?

4 Read this letter to a supermarket manager.

> The Manager
> Shoprite Supermarket
>
> Dear Sir/Madam
> When I was in your *supermarket this week* I found *Hair Beauty shampoo for sale*. This *shampoo has palm oil in it*. This is bad for the rainforest, because *people cut down rainforest trees to make palm oil plantations*. I would like to ask you to *stop selling this shampoo*. If a lot of people do this, *it will save some of the rainforest*. Yours faithfully,
> Anna Ortiz

Now write a letter of your own, to a supermarket, or a shop, or an office, and ask them to change something that they are doing. Change the words in *italics* to make a new letter.

5 Find some more information about a person or organization that works for the rainforest, and make a poster or give a talk to your class. Here are some websites that can help you.

Dian Fossey Gorilla Fund International: www.gorillafund.org

Raincoast Conservation Society: www.raincoast.org

Green Belt Movement (GBM): www.greenbeltmovement.org

Orangutan Foundation International: www.orangutan.org

Rainforest Foundation: www.rainforestfoundation.org

WWF: www.wwf.org

Greenpeace: www.greenpeace.org/international

ABOUT THE AUTHOR

Rowena Akinyemi is British, and after many years in Africa, she now lives and works in Cambridge, though she still goes to Africa every year on holiday. She has worked in English Language Teaching for twenty-five years, in Africa and Britain, and has been writing ELT fiction for fifteen years. She has written several other stories for the Oxford Bookworms Library, including *Nelson Mandela* (Factfiles) and *Love or Money?* (Crime and Mystery). She has also adapted several stories for the same series, and her adaptation of *Cry Freedom* was a finalist in the Language Learner Literature Award, an international award for ELT readers, in 2004. She has also written books for children.

She has four children and is a keen football fan, supporting Manchester United. She also enjoys country holidays in Britain – a long walk over hills or along cliffs in Wales, followed by a cream tea in a village teashop. But she also enjoys days in London shopping, walking on Hampstead Heath, looking at historical buildings, going to a concert or the theatre. She likes all sorts of music, especially African music, jazz, classical music, and Bob Dylan, and enjoys reading crime fiction and biographies.

OXFORD BOOKWORMS LIBRARY

Classics • Crime & Mystery • Factfiles • Fantasy & Horror
Human Interest • Playscripts • Thriller & Adventure
True Stories • World Stories

The OXFORD BOOKWORMS LIBRARY provides enjoyable reading in English, with a wide range of classic and modern fiction, non-fiction, and plays. It includes original and adapted texts in seven carefully graded language stages, which take learners from beginner to advanced level. An overview is given on the next pages.

All Stage 1 titles are available as audio recordings, as well as over eighty other titles from Starter to Stage 6. All Starters and many titles at Stages 1 to 4 are specially recommended for younger learners. Every Bookworm is illustrated, and Starters and Factfiles have full-colour illustrations.

The OXFORD BOOKWORMS LIBRARY also offers extensive support. Each book contains an introduction to the story, notes about the author, a glossary, and activities. Additional resources include tests and worksheets, and answers for these and for the activities in the books. There is advice on running a class library, using audio recordings, and the many ways of using Oxford Bookworms in reading programmes. Resource materials are available on the website <www.oup.com/elt/bookworms>.

The *Oxford Bookworms Collection* is a series for advanced learners. It consists of volumes of short stories by well-known authors, both classic and modern. Texts are not abridged or adapted in any way, but carefully selected to be accessible to the advanced student.

You can find details and a full list of titles in the *Oxford Bookworms Library Catalogue* and *Oxford English Language Teaching Catalogues*, and on the website <www.oup.com/elt/bookworms>.

THE OXFORD BOOKWORMS LIBRARY
GRADING AND SAMPLE EXTRACTS

STARTER • 250 HEADWORDS

present simple – present continuous – imperative –
can/cannot, must – *going to* (future) – simple gerunds ...

Her phone is ringing – but where is it?

Sally gets out of bed and looks in her bag. No phone. She looks under the bed. No phone. Then she looks behind the door. There is her phone. Sally picks up her phone and answers it. *Sally's Phone*

STAGE 1 • 400 HEADWORDS

... past simple – coordination with *and, but, or* –
subordination with *before, after, when, because, so* ...

I knew him in Persia. He was a famous builder and I worked with him there. For a time I was his friend, but not for long. When he came to Paris, I came after him – I wanted to watch him. He was a very clever, very dangerous man. *The Phantom of the Opera*

STAGE 2 • 700 HEADWORDS

... present perfect – *will* (future) – *(don't) have to, must not, could* –
comparison of adjectives – simple *if* clauses – past continuous –
tag questions – *ask/tell* + infinitive ...

While I was writing these words in my diary, I decided what to do. I must try to escape. I shall try to get down the wall outside. The window is high above the ground, but I have to try. I shall take some of the gold with me – if I escape, perhaps it will be helpful later. *Dracula*

STAGE 3 • 1000 HEADWORDS
... should, may – present perfect continuous – *used to* – past perfect
– causative – relative clauses – indirect statements ...

Of course, it was most important that no one should see Colin, Mary, or Dickon entering the secret garden. So Colin gave orders to the gardeners that they must all keep away from that part of the garden in future. *The Secret Garden*

STAGE 4 • 1400 HEADWORDS
... past perfect continuous – passive (simple forms) –
would conditional clauses – indirect questions –
relatives with *where/when* – gerunds after prepositions/phrases ...

I was glad. Now Hyde could not show his face to the world again. If he did, every honest man in London would be proud to report him to the police. *Dr Jekyll and Mr Hyde*

STAGE 5 • 1800 HEADWORDS
... future continuous – future perfect –
passive (modals, continuous forms) –
would have conditional clauses – modals + perfect infinitive ...

If he had spoken Estella's name, I would have hit him. I was so angry with him, and so depressed about my future, that I could not eat the breakfast. Instead I went straight to the old house. *Great Expectations*

STAGE 6 • 2500 HEADWORDS
... passive (infinitives, gerunds) – advanced modal meanings –
clauses of concession, condition

When I stepped up to the piano, I was confident. It was as if I knew that the prodigy side of me really did exist. And when I started to play, I was so caught up in how lovely I looked that I didn't worry how I would sound. *The Joy Luck Club*

BOOKWORMS · FACTFILES · STAGE 2
Seasons and Celebrations
JACKIE MAGUIRE

In English-speaking countries around the world people celebrate Easter, Valentine's Day, Christmas, and other special days. Some celebrations are new, like Remembrance Day and Mother's Day; others, like the summer solstice, go back thousands of years.

What happens on these special days? What do people eat, where do they go, what do they do? Why is there a special day for eating pancakes? Who is the 'guy' that children take onto the streets in November? And where do many people like to spend the shortest night of the year in England? Come on a journey through a year of celebrations, from New Year's Eve to Christmas.

BOOKWORMS · FACTFILES · STAGE 2
Ireland
TIM VICARY

There are many different Irelands. There is the Ireland of peaceful rivers, green fields, and beautiful islands. There is the Ireland of song and dance, pubs and theatres – the country of James Joyce, Bob Geldof, and Riverdance. And there is the Ireland of guns, fighting, death, and the hope of peace. Come with us and visit all of these Irelands – and many more . . .